God POCKETS-(AWww/God)

God POCKETS-(AWww/God)

Purposes of courageous knowledge encouragement through scriptures of A Woman walking with God-(AWww/God)

JANIS A. JACKSON

iUniverse, Inc.
Bloomington

God POCKETS-(AWww/God)
Purposes of courageous knowledge encouragement through scriptures of A
Woman walking with God-(AWww/God)

iUniverse books may be ordered through booksellers or by contacting:

iUniverse
1663 Liberty Drive
Bloomington, IN 47403
www.iuniverse.com
1-800-Authors (1-800-288-4677)

ISBN: 978-1-4620-2638-8 (sc)
ISBN: 978-1-4620-2639-5 (ebk)

Library of Congress Control Number: 2011913042

Printed in the United States of America

iUniverse rev. date: 10/18/2011

ACKNOWLEDGMENTS AND DEDICATION

I am so thankful to my Lord and Savior Jesus Christ who has given me the divine inspirational words through the Holy Spirit to write this book.

To all who have supported, encouraged and promoted this project from its known conception to birth:

My Husband
My Parents
My Daughter
My Stepchildren
My Brothers
My (Cuzzy's) Cousins
My Aunts and Uncles
My Pastor
My Friends

A special thanks to my cuzzy Adoria, and my friend Kim who always gave their ear, encouragement and excitement, and to my grand daughter, Carrah-Ahlyse who is growing strong.

In addition, I am so grateful and thankful to God to <u>all</u> my long time friends, prayer partners, encouragers and supporters who have all prayed, listened, directed, labored, and patiently waited for me to finish this book.

Have a Thankful Day!
This is the day the Lord has made; we will rejoice and be glad in it.
Psalms 118:24

This book is lovingly dedicated to the many fond memories made with all of my beloved family and friends while on earth before they departed to heaven. Many of who provided and surrounded me with so much love, attention, wisdom, spiritual guidance, help, fun and friendship. For this I am grateful and I give glory to God.

FOREWORD

Over 25 years ago, I met the author of God POCKETS-A Woman walking with God. I was barely 19 and she was about 23. At that time, we both were married with one child, both daughters. My daughter, being the oldest was almost 2 years old, and her daughter was about 10 months. Neither of us knew that when we first met it would result in my opportunity to experience some of the inspirations written in this book. Throughout the years we had so many similarities, which I believe is what drew us together to become the best of friends and sisters, even today.

Through many years of us sharing our lunch, our thoughts, difficulties, prayer requests, dialoguing about life issues, our children, our families, our jobs, our achievements, shopping, dreams of writing books and most of all communicating and experiencing God's goodness and greatness. Yes God's greatness. Both of us have encountered tragedies in our lives, the sudden death of her daughter's father, and when I lost my oldest daughter to sickle cell, when she was 23. You get that "23" the same age the author was when I met her. Over and over God's greatness is apparent time and time again. I was there then for her, she helped me, and is still encouraging me through the difficulty of my eldest daughter's death. I believe the inspirations from God POCKETS-A Woman walking with God, are encouragement too.

We always thought I would be the first one to write my book, considering my dreams to write, and my whole life being a living testimony. Significantly, this number 23 is the author's birth date, March 23, and her favorite number is 23. Also, my birth date is 2 months and 3 days from her birthday. Notice how the similarities occur with us, and our lives have paralleled in so many ways.

Let's look at a few of the similarities:

The Author
Worked in same department when we met
Maternal grandmother passed away in 80's
Home church fellowshipped together
When we first met married with one daughter/their dad's born in September
Daughter born November 9 and favorite color purple
Born March 23
Have two siblings
Mother worked and retired from same company
Father in law/stepdaughter born May 26
Worked in same department 1987-1989
Retiring from the same company
Writing a book
Not tall in height

Mine
Worked in same department when we met
Maternal grandmother passed away in 80's
Home church fellowshipped together
When we first met married with one daughter/their dad's born in September
Daughter born November 21 and favorite color purple
My sister born March 30, my brother born March 22
Have two siblings
Mother worked and retired from same company
Born May 26
Worked in same department 1987-1989
Retiring from the same company 3 years after she retires
Writing a book
Not tall in height

I believe when you begin to read God POCKETS-A Woman walking with God, you will see how God's great plan, and purposes, unfold in so many ways. You will begin to see that this book, God POCKETS-A Woman walking with God, was indeed derived when we first met years ago. God POCKETS-A Woman walking with God truly exemplifies evidence of a woman spending time with God, and studying the word of God daily. God POCKETS-A Woman walking with God also provides expressions of knowledge, applications of wisdom with scriptures, and worksheet questions. It's not just another devotional, but a thought provoking and easy to read book. You will find how a few minutes spent each day studying the word of God enhances your knowledge of God's word, equips you in your walk with God, and encourages your heart.

God POCKETS-A Woman walking with God is written by a woman who truly demonstrates a woman spending time with the Lord daily, and writing the vision given to her from God. Women of all ages will find something for themselves and their love ones as they travel on their journey with the Lord. Others also will agree that God POCKETS-A Woman walking with God will appeal to all regardless of race, age, creed or color.

(By Monique R. Smith)
(Thank you Monique)

INTRODUCTION

What is God POCKETS-AWww/God? God POCKETS is God's purposes of courageous knowledge encouragement through scriptures, and AWww/God is A Woman walking with God. In 2007 I made a resolution that I would get up earlier to read and study the word of God everyday. My goal was to read one chapter a day and completely read the entire bible within a year. Around the end of January 2008, I was still up early reading and studying the word before work, but I was nowhere close to completing the task I had assigned to myself. I don't remember where I stopped in the New Testament. I had several other responsibilities at the time.

After I would read a chapter in the bible, God would reveal the divine daily inspirations of wisdom to me. Since my gift from God is the gift of encouragement, I began sending the daily encouraging text messages early to my daughter as a wake up call and daily communication to her. She was living on her own, so this was also my way of communicating to her that I wanted to see if she was awake and up for work.

I continued doing this for several months, and I would pray and ask God to direct me to whom else I needed to send the text messages also. In December 2009, the Holy Spirit said start adding a scripture with the text messages. In January 2010, I began sending a text message Monday through Friday with a scripture at the end of it. I figured everyone needed or wanted a break from all my text messages on the weekends.

Several more months passed and the Holy Spirit was giving me inspiration after inspiration after inspiration. Now it became a challenge to find a scripture to go along with the text message everyday. I pulled out the dictionary, the concordance, my bible handbook and several other versions of the bible. It looked like a library on the bed. I had no idea where God was leading me, I was just going along with Him, and getting closer to Him from studying the word each day. It was stabilizing and strengthening me because the last few years had taken a lot out of me. On June 14, 2010 I sent a text message that said, "You may overlook God's word, but you cannot ignore God"-read Haggai 1:7-9 and 2:17-19. This was probably one of many clues that the Holy Spirit was directing me to begin writing, because again on July 28, 2010 I sent another text message that said, "Don't just dream know the vision"-read Habakkuk 2:2-3. I guess I was too excited about our upcoming vacation in July 2010 that I just missed those previous clues all together.

God has such a sense of humor so after vacation was over, and I was back at work, in August 2010, the Holy Spirit spoke to me again and said, "Write the vision." With that direction more divine inspirations were being birthed out of me daily. During the next couple of weeks part of the title was uttered. On August 27, 2010, I was at work thinking about the word POCKETS. I sent out a text message to a few family and friends, and asked them to give me some words for each letter in the word POCKETS, but I never told them what it was regarding. Nevertheless, I received several responses back. After receiving the instructions for this vision God was pointing me to and praying over what POCKETS meant to me, I wrote on a piece of paper inside my tablet God POCKETS-God's purposes of courageous knowledge encouragement through scriptures. Then I wrote the words "crazy" and "outrageous", and I thought to myself that is exactly what some people may think of me; however, it doesn't matter because I am content in the Lord, I take comfort in walking with God in the word, I am confident with God, and growing closer to Him each day. What matters more to me is what God thinks of me, and my obedience to Him.

I had written several notes in a notebook tablet. I also had several questions too. Then the Holy Spirit said "talk to your Pastor." At this point only God knew what all the notes, words and writing I was doing was all about.

One day I was making some business cards on the computer for my cousin and started playing around with putting together the postcards below.

I placed the order unbeknownst to me, that this was exactly what I was to do. The postcards arrived in the mail and I just put them aside. Again the spirit of God spoke to me and said, "You need to talk to your Pastor". I thought to myself I haven't talked anyone about this. I also thought I had to figure out how to end my own fear and get enough courage to tell someone.

This was my very own first super step of faith to exercise my own God POCKETS-A Woman walking with God experience. Yes my God given gift is encouragement, but most of the time I never had to say anything to use my gift. One night while writing some notes, I sent my daughter a text message that I was writing a book. She was excited and asked me "what did my husband say." I responded back that I had not told him yet and that she should not tell him either. One of my cousins figured out that I must have been writing something, so I told her a little bit about it.

Again the spirit of God spoke to me and said, "You need to talk to your Pastor".

If you really know me, I am a very shy person, and when I really express something that is important to me or something that I feel very strongly about, I get emotional. I don't talk much and I just didn't know how it would be received about me writing a book. Growing up I never liked to mention what I had or what I did because some people did not understand. They received it as bragging, they didn't believe you, or they hated you for what you had or even looked like. I was singled out so much growing up for being what others perceived as being a certain way, not being a certain way, looking a certain way, living where I lived, and the list goes on. This fear had lived with me a long, long, long time.

One night while I was writing some notes, I told my husband. It appeared that he only heard half of what I said. He didn't say much that particular night. A day or so later we talked about it again and he said to me "that God would not have given me this assignment, if it was not already inside of me." I was very moved by this comment out of my husband's mouth. Later the Holy Spirit confirmed to me that when I told him he was exhausted from working, but that he heard exactly what I told him, he just had to digest it all about me writing a book. Also the Holy Spirit said I needed to reveal this to a few other people. I began thinking again how do I tell them, and whom do I tell this to next. Why did I have this fear?

God is so good at how He puts everything together. I remember this particular day so vividly on Friday, October 1, 2010 when I was leaving the church, my path crossed directly in line of the Pastor. Regardless to whether I was obedient, God made it so easy for me to do what he had already asked me to do. When I spoke to my Pastor, we talked briefly about how the family was doing because it was the same day of one of my cousin's funeral service that I was attending. As I was walking away I said quickly as I possibly could, "I need to set up an appointment to meet with you, regarding something the Holy Spirit is leading me to do". He said OK.

I was not ignoring God initially, I was just afraid of how it would be received that I was writing a book. You see how God prepared me on the path and directed me on what He wanted me to do. All that was required was my obedience to Him, and to remove my thinking about myself, and just rely on His guidance and direction.

I love how the Good News Bible version of Psalms 23:1-4 reads *The Lord is my Shepherd; I have everything I need. He lets me rest in fields of green grass and leads me to quiet pools of fresh water. He gives me new strength. He guides me in right paths, as He has promised. Even if I go through the deepest darkness, I will not be afraid, Lord for you are with me. Your Shepherd's rod and staff protect me. This is exactly what I believe the Lord was saying to me in these scriptures.* **Because I am the Lord your Shepherd, I have everything you need. As you are walking you can rest assure and be led by Me, and I will give you new strength, because I am guiding you in the right path just as I have promised, and no matter if you have to go through even the deepest darkness, you will not be afraid, because I am with you, protecting you.**

Even though I still had to encourage myself, I knew I needed to set up the meeting with my Pastor especially now. Well two more weeks passed before I finally asked the church secretary to schedule me for a meeting with my Pastor. On October 26, 2010 I met with my Pastor and during that meeting I explained to him what I had been working on. He shared information with me, and some of the things he had to do while writing his books, and also prayed with me.

God POCKETS is simply God's instruction, direction of simple applications and encouragements. I pray that it will motivate you to the following:

- Enhance your knowledge of the word of God and apply it in your daily life
- Elevate your interest in the word of God
- Excite your spirit through daily study of the word of God
- Encourage your heart through the word of God, even when it seems things are going from bad to worse
- Establish your faith and let go of your fears using the word of God
- Embrace your belief in God
- Express your difficulties and or struggles to God to get over them
- Engage in your obedience to the word of God
- Emphasize your standards through the word of God
- Expand your own God-given gifts and talents through the word of God
- Experience achieving an obtainable goal with God
- Evaluate your skills and abilities for God's purpose
- Enlarge your confidence through the word of God
- Encore of praise for God's grace
- Emerge your understanding of God's purpose for your life
- Excite your commitment to serve God
- Endow your power through the word of God

I pray this will be a book you read over, and over, and over, and over again. I also pray when you read God POCKETS-A Woman walking with God you will discover or utilize your God given purpose, be determined to understand God's promises, desire to uncover God's plan, and diligently unleash God's power, that will help you during your daily walk with God.

TABLE OF CONTENTS

A Woman walking with God daily

Colossians 1:10-12

A woman walking with God daily follows the will of God for directions in her life. She submits to the will of God. She is a woman who listens to God, and hears God speak to her through the word. She is a woman who is happy doing the will of God. She never wanders or wavers from God because she is certain He is her shepherd, He will always lead her according to His will, He will be with her, and keep her safe.

A woman walking with God daily admits to her own weaknesses, and confesses her wrongs to Him. She is a woman who asks God for forgiveness and accepts that God has forgiven her when she asks. She understands God's constant love for her. She is a woman who gives God praise for His forgiveness, given to her through the blood of Jesus Christ sacrificed on the cross.

A woman walking with God daily is devoted to daily prayer. She sincerely pours out her heart to God about all of her concerns. She is a woman who prays continuously. She communicates to God about every issue, every need, every struggle, every matter, every desire of her heart, and even her fears. She is a woman, when she prays to God, is convinced that no bargaining is necessary. She is a woman that is sure that God hears all of her prayers, and comforted that God will answer her prayers according to His will.

A woman walking with God daily is obedient to doing the will of God, by acknowledging the plans of God, and walking in the ways of God. She is a woman praying to God, worshipping God, and praising God in everything. She is confident that through her obedience that God will work on her behalf. She is a woman who listens to receive God's divine instructions, and she is content with accepting the instructions given to her from God.

A woman walking with God daily is totally committed to God. She is encouraged and convinced of God's promises, even if she has to wait awhile for God to answer. She is a woman constantly dependent on God, because she knows that God will give her success in everything.

A woman walking with God daily is seeking to do the work of God, and gives of her time and talents to be available to serve Him. She is thankful and grateful to God for she knows every gift God has given to her. She withstands and keeps her faith strong in God, even at her worst. She is a woman that loves God with her whole heart, all of her mind, all of her body, all of her might, and all of her soul.

A woman walking with God daily is so sensitive to the spirit of God, and puts all of her trust in God. She is a woman who knows God is faithful and can be fully trusted. She is a woman who influences others for God. She is a woman serving God and motivated in sharing God's word with all.

A woman walking with God daily sometimes must wait to hear from God. She worships God while she waits, and she knows that God is worthy of all of her worship. She is a woman, who is satisfied with waiting to hear from her God. She is a woman even if she is weeping, she continues worshipping God, and keeps waiting for Him to provide her an answer.

A woman walking with God daily walks willingly with the Lord. She is a woman who believes God will walk along with her. She is a woman who is secure that God will always be on her side and will never fail her.

A woman walking with God daily studies the word of God, and takes time out to spend with God daily so she can hear the voice of God, through His word. She understands her strength is definitely found in the word of God. She is a woman whose life reveals the ways of God.

A woman walking with God daily is an extra ordinary woman. She is a woman of God who is obedient, grateful, available, directed, forgiving, diligent, encouraged, happy, devoted, humble, sensitive, joyful, motivated, thankful, patient, committed, disciplined, worshipping, merciful, trusting, mindful, gracious, virtuous, self controlled, positive, sincere, understanding, submissive, confident, victorious, optimistic and zealous in the will, work and ways of the Lord.

A Woman walking w/God – ("AWww/God") daily and writing the vision

Which woman walking with God are you?

A Woman walking with God is willing to walk in the will of God. *Read Psalms 119:1 and 3 and II Corinthians 5:7*

A Woman walking with God is a woman waiting to hear divine instructions from the Lord through the word. *Read Genesis 49:18, Psalms 27:10, Psalms 37:9 and Isaiah 40:31*

A Woman walking with God is a woman watching to see God work. *Read Psalms 102:7, Proverbs 8:34, Matthew 25:13, Mark 13:37 and Colossians 4:2*

A Woman walking with God is a woman working through the word of God. *Read Isaiah 1:19, John 9:4 and James 2:17*

A Woman walking with God walks willingly with the Lord. *Read Jeremiah 32:38-41 and Hebrews 6:3*

A Woman walking with God does not wander or waver from the ways of the Lord. *Read Hebrew 10:23 and Romans 4:20*

A Woman walking with God withstands in God's will, even at her worst. *Read Luke 21:15 and I Peter 5:9*

A Woman walking with God witnesses the miracles of God. *Read Proverbs 14:5, I John 5:7-8 and I John 5:9*

A Woman walking with God withstands, even if she is weeping. *Read Luke 21:15 and I Peter 5:9*

A Woman walking with God hears from God, while she is reading and studying the word. *Read Luke 11:28, Romans 10:17, I Thessalonians 4:11 and II Timothy 2:15*

A Woman walking with God is a woman who worships, while she is waiting for God.
Read Psalms 96:9, Psalms 99:5 and John 4:24

A Woman walking with God is willing to wait for God, after she has asked Him to direct her in what's next.
Read Matthew 6:6-8 and 32-33, Matthew 7:7, John 11:22 and James 1:5

Janis A. Jackson

ABC's of "AWww/God"

A-Available-1 Corinthians 15:58

B-Believe-Acts 16:31

C-Committed-Proverbs 16:3

D-Directed/Diligent-Proverbs 3:6 and Proverbs 4:23

E-Encouraged-1 Thessalonians 5:14

F-Faithful-Luke 16:10

G-Grateful-Lamentation 3:41

H-Humble/Holiness-Psalms 113:6, Romans 1:4 and Hebrews 12:10

I-Instruction-Proverbs 8:33

J-Joyful-Psalms 100:1

K-Kept-I Peter 1:5

L-Listen-Acts 13:16

M-Motivated-1 Thessalonians 2:4

N-New/Newborn-Roman 6:4 and 2 Corinthians 5:17

O-Obedient/Optimistic-Isaiah 1:19 and 1 Peter 1:14

P-Patient/Positive/Prays/Praise-Ecclesiastes 7:8, Psalms 40:1, Psalms 150, Luke 18:1, 1 Thessalonians 5:17

Q-Quiet-I Peter 3:4, 1 Thessalonians 4:11

R-Rejoice-1 Thessalonians 5:16

S-Sincere/Sensitive/Sacrifice/Stand still-Luke 21:19, 1 Corinthians 16:13, 1 Thessalonians 5:18, 1 Timothy 1:5

T-Truthful/Thankful/Trustworthy-Proverbs 3:5, Proverbs 16:11, 1 Corinthians 7:25 and 1 Thessalonians 5:18

U-Understanding-Proverbs 4:5, Proverbs 19:8 and James 5:8

V-Virtuous-Proverbs 31

W-Willing/Worships-John 4:24

X-Extraordinary/Exalt-Psalms 99:2, Psalms 113:4

Y-Yield-1 Peter 2:9

Z-Zealous-Read Titus 2:14

Ask God for what you want

Stop telling God what you want and start asking Him-*read Matthew 7:7*

When you have questions, ask God for the answers to what's next regarding His will for you. If you ask man a lot of questions, he may become agitated. God assures us what we ask; He will do what we ask according to His will. God encourages us to come before Him and ask, when we do He always provides answers to us-*read Isaiah 7:11-14, 58:2, Luke 20:21, John 11:22 and James 1:5*

Just follow my lead

Oh my God this was such a revelation word to me. One day my husband was leaving for work and we were discussing some plans and I made the comment that I think we should wait, and before he walked out the door, he said to me "just follow my lead." When you can follow God's lead, you can trust Him fully. You let go of what you think you know, and what you think you can do, and let God take full control of you. He only asks us to trust in Him, so we can follow His direction.

When you trust in the Lord with all of your heart and do not lean to your own understanding, you can truly just follow the Lord's lead in everything and always.

Read Proverbs 3:5-6
(Thank you to my husband)

Let me tell my story

God has already written your entire story. The story of you is not about you alone. God wrote your story before you were ever conceived. God promised to take care of you, to be with you, and never forsake you during your story. God will give you prosperity and health in your story. God has peace for you within your story. God gives provision throughout your story. God answers your prayers during your story. God prepares you for your next story line. God proves himself to you over and over again within your story. Even when the enemy seeks to pursue you in your story, God is always a part of the story.

Life is usually unfair and there are things we don't deserve, but what we sow grace is there to grip us tight and thank God it does. We may not always do everything correctly; however, if we just do our portion, we don't have to worry about if God will do His part.

In order to recover you must remove the stone. Whatever the matter, concern or issue is, you must uncover it. You got to face it and open it up. Whether it is fear of failing or falling, rejection, low self-esteem, addictions, lying, stealing, negativism, cheating, overeating you will always be bound by the fear, if you don't loose it and let go of it.

God has to remove you from your comfort zone. We can get too comfortable and become complacent if we do not get out of those places where we are so familiar with or so comfortable.

Here's how to walk in your story:

- Remove all distractions
- Release your fears

- Repent and ask God to help you accept your present story now so that you can recover, and be restored from your past story
- Respond positively to your life story
- Recognize whatever it is you need to recover from your past story
- Replace whatever your test is with a testimony—tell your story
- Resist the devil and he will flee-tell the enemy to go and let him leave
- Rejoice in the Lord that you recovered, and you are walking in newness in your story
- Receive Jesus Christ as your personal Savior
- Revive your personal bible study

I know our story can be uncomfortable, but we can actually excel in the unknown thru Jesus Christ during our story. You don't need to tell every detail of your story to everyone, but do make sure your story honors God. *Read Psalms 26:7*

Waiting for your Boaz

You don't want to waste time with Bozo, you want to wait for Boaz. So remember don't waste your time with a Bozo, so you can spend a lifetime with a Boaz-*read Ruth 2:4-17 and Ruth 4:1-10*

You can be single and satisfied and saved without settling-*read Hebrews 13:4*

Sometimes there are things we must give up to get to God, or get to where God wants us to be—*read Luke 9:25 and I Timothy 6:6*

Satan doesn't mind us embracing (accepting) more information, he just don't want us engaging (acting/applying) on any of the applications—*read Proverbs 2:1-2, Ecclesiastes 12:13, Romans 2:13, Ephesians 4:11-15 and 11:6-10 and James 1:22-25*

Pray don't play—*read Luke 18:1 and 27, James 5:16*

Some times you must wait for you what you want—*read Psalms 91:15, Proverbs 3:5-6, II Corinthians 12:9, Philippians 4:19*

It won't be good, if it is not all God,—*read Hebrews 13:21, James 1:17*

A Lady

Just because you are a woman, you MUST always remember to be a lady. Just being female, being a grown woman, or being a woman, does not make you a lady. A lady is godly. A lady has virtue. A lady is true to her faith in God. A lady is reverent to God's will. So be a lady and not just a woman. *Read Proverbs 31*

Which woman are you?

Are you a woman of giving-*read 1 Timothy 4:15*

Are you a woman of grief-*read Hebrews 13:17*

Are you a woman of gratefulness-*read Psalms 147:7*

Are you a woman of godliness-*read 2 Peter 1:6 and 2 Timothy 3:12*

Are you a woman of guilt-*read Psalms 38:4*

Are you a woman of genuineness-*read 1 Peter 1:7*

Are you a woman of grace-*read 2 Peter 3:18*

Are you a woman of gladness-*read Psalms 100:2*

Are you a woman of greed-*read Luke 11:39*

Are you a woman of goals-*read Philippians 3:14*

Are you a woman of glory-*read 1 Peter 4:14*

Are you a woman of gentleness-*read 1 Peter 2:18 and Titus 3:2*

Don't hide your blessing

Don't worry about your haters-God said don't hide your blessing.

What God has already predestined, predetermined, or preplanned for you, it is already prepared for you and it is yours. It has your name on it and no one else can get it, but you. This is why we have to be so careful to give God the honor, glory and praise that are due to Him.

Read Psalms 84:11 says for Jehovah God is a sun and shield; Jehovah will give grace and glory no good thing will he withhold from them that walk uprightly.

When you are blessed by God or receive a blessing from God, I don't think anyone would say "oh no that's okay I don't want a blessing."

When you are obedient and diligent about the will of God, your blessing will come upon you and overtake you. God has already promised this, and there is nothing you can do about it, except to be obedient and accept the will of God. So you don't have to worry about your haters. God has already established you for Him.

Haters do not understand your blessings. Haters don't understand your story. Haters are immature regarding the will of God.
Read Deuteronomy 28:3-10, I Chronicles 16:8-12, Psalms 103:1-2 and Romans 1:30

God's KISS

God provides security and it is genuine. You are kept in spiritual strength-*read Psalms 16:9 and Proverbs 10:30*

Total Marriage Commitment-Don't just build your household but be a home holder

Even with challenges there must be total commitment between the married couple circle called "US". It is no longer I or U, but now its "US" or "WE". Total marriage commitment is precious to the purpose of the marriage. Because God advised and commanded marriage, therefore God created marriage to be a ministry. In *Ephesians 5:31 God said a man shall leave his mother and father and he should be joined to his wife and the two shall become one.* It does not say the man will be joined with a friend or friends so in order to maintain a commitment, there must be constant communication and lots of couple time everyday. There should NEVER BE any other FRIENDSHIPS that you cleave to over your own spouse. If there is, this could be creating a breeding ground for a risky marriage relationship. Marriage should be based upon vows. **Successful marriages base their relationship on their vows, not their voyages.**

It is my prayer for every married couple to develop a MORE motivated and meaningful marriage. In order for wives to follow their husbands, husbands must follow God in **every** area; however, wives must follow God regardless. Couples "MUST" strive together for excellence in living, in character, and within their marriage life together in order to have a successful marriage. There must be NO secrets, but ONLY sharing with each other after praying together, between every marriage couple.

Households must come together as home holders. We must learn to build our own households and be a home holder. The ONLY way to build your marriage is to allow God to be the head of your house. It is not enough to just be a couple. Any man and woman can do that. For couples to be blessed by God in their home, they MUST be married, and they MUST be obedient to God in their marriage. There must be no competition among married couples only comfort from each other. Satan seeks to divide MARRIED couples any way he can. The enemy knows marriage is honorable to God. Now to build a house it takes nails, beams, sheetrock, bricks, wood etc., but to build the marriage home it takes total commitment first to God, to each other, love, total honesty, trust, consideration, communication, compassion, confession, comforting, harmony, understanding, apologies, and unbroken covenant. There is usually love (especially in the beginning), but honesty and harmony are often missing. There MUST be friendship not friction and never any fighting, continuous dedication to God in marriage no division. When you say "I DO", to have total marriage success, requires remaining in love with each other, no fault finding, and striving daily to put in practice that stick togetherness everyday, no matter what even if you disagree, and sharing in the marriage promises and vows <u>ONLY</u> to each other, as you promised before God when you said "I DO". God blesses marriages of men and women in their marriage, through their commitment of their marriage vows.

Married couples MUST continually put ONLY their own spouse first, not second, and not last in the marriage circle. There is nothing broken in a complete circle. That's why when VOWS are exchanged and rings are given, it is EXTREMELY important to remember rings should always be worn as a constant reminder of the unbroken marriage commitment circle that was made. So many people say a ring doesn't make you married, but a ring is a SIGNIFICANT SYMBOL of importance in the marriage commitment circle. What a ring says is: YES, I AM MARRIED. I AM REMINDED DAILY OF THE MARRIAGE COMMITMENT I MADE TO GOD, AND MY SPOUSE. MY MARRIAGE CIRCLE IS SEALED AND WILL BE BLESSED BECAUSE I AM IN AN HONORABLE CONVENANT WITH GOD AND MY ONE SPOUSE THAT I MARRIED.

Why are some people so uncomfortable with doing what God says to do within the marriage circle, and sooooooooooooooooooooooooooooo comfortable in doing what God has said DO NOT do like having friendly or casual conversations with those single acquaintenances who are not your spouse and your spouse knows nothing about the individual, having just friendly conversations that often open the door to create trouble, having affairs, flings, and now with technology all other types of communicating and socializing outside of the marriage circle. There must be daily prayer together, hugs and submission <u>only</u> to one another to build and keep the lifetime commitment of promise within the marriage.

Within a successful marriage you have to remove all unhealthy relationships, issues of lust, and any other distractions that tend to bring discord. There MUST <u>always</u> be accountability, availability, acceptance, and acknowledgement for the man and woman who said 'I DO' to a lifetime of marriage.
Read Matthew 19:6

Remember this: God left the man in charge, and head of the household. When God saw everything He made and it was good, He saw that Adam needed one wife not several friends. When married couples are in God, they can be confident that God led them together and they will be led continually together in God, until death! God joins two together to become one and only one with Him to fulfill his purpose. *Read Proverbs 31:10*

A respectable Man wants a respected Woman and when he finds her, he makes her honest and marries her-**read Genesis 2:24, Deuteronomy 10:20 and 30:20, Joshua 23:2, Psalms 119:31, Proverbs 18:22, and Matthew 19:4-6**

Tests

Don't worry about your test-it will be a testimony for you-*read Luke 21:13-15*

The way you talk tells a lot about your testimony.
Tests help to develop us.
Tests disclose what we don't know.
Tests divulge what we have done.
Tests describe what we may still need to do.
Tests determine what we have learned.

Stop trying to put God in a Box

There is boldness out of the box
God is not limited to only one place
So why are we unlimited to move from our space
Whatever you face
God gives you grace
To run the race
So stay in your place
Just keep the pace
And a smile on your face
Because God's faithfulness you can always trace.

Read Lamentations 3:23, Hebrews 12:26-28 and I John 5:14-15

God is just like that

There were many days I thought to myself "I am not sending anymore of these texts, because it is probably annoying to most anyway". On August 11, 2010 I failed to send the text message, as I usually would have to one of my long time prayer sister buddies. I was walking down the hallway at work and the spirit prompted me to send this message: **Until you have a vision to move ahead, you will always live in yesterday's struggles. You have to ask God what lesson you need to learn**-*read James 4:6-8*

Shortly afterwards, I received a response back that said, "call me." Immediately in my mind I'm thinking "oh my" what's happening. So when I made the call, she tells me how the spirit is working and that when she received the message, it was just right on time for her.

I am so thankful to God that this vision is not only His will for me, but it is His work also. Whether I am obedient to God's will, His will would be done; therefore, His purpose has be priority once it has been ordered or ordained.

"Have a faith-filled, motivated, positive, and productive day"
(Thank you Kattie)

Don't trip, don't flip, and don't slip

Don't trip because God has a purpose for you, and it may cause your lips to become unzipped.

Don't flip because God has a plan for you, and it may cause your thoughts to get ripped.

Don't slip because God has a promise for you, and it may cause your actions to make you dip, or your attitude to strip or snip.

<u>So remember this tip</u>: Don't trip because you may get trapped, don't flip because you may fall, and don't slip because you may sin.

Don't be tempted, just trust-don't trip
Don't fret have faith-don't flip
Don't sweat, be still—don't slip
God can and God will

Read Psalms 17:3-5, Proverbs, 23:7, Proverbs 24:1 and Jude 1:24

How to obtain an achievable goal in 30 days

Philippians 3:12-15 and Philippians 4:13

1. *Define exactly what your goal is.*
2. *Begin each day in prayer regarding your goal.*
3. *Is this a goal that you can accomplish for God?*
4. *Is this a goal God wants you to accomplish for Him?*
5. *Is the goal obtainable and reasonable for you to achieve within 30 days?*
6. *Do you know what you need to do to obtain the goal?*
7. *Make a daily to do list for the goal you want to achieve.*
8. *At the end of each day, journal if you accomplished the goal for that day. If not, list why not.*

Below are a few examples of achievable goals:

- *Get up 30 minutes earlier each day to read the bible*
- *Take 30 minutes at the end of each day after work or school to sit down and relax*
- *Start a regular workout/exercise program*
- *Lose weight*
- *Fast one day a week for 30 days*
- *Win one soul to Christ a month*
- *Leave for work 15 minutes earlier each day to avoid rushing, traffic, delays, etc.*
- *Give up television three times a week*
- *Eat healthier*
- *Save one dollar a day*
- *Pray with your spouse/family/child/children/grandchildren everyday*
- *Clean out your closets and remove everything you have not used, can't wear in the past 3 years*
- *Eat one meal in the kitchen with your spouse/family/child/children/grandchildren without watching television everyday*
- *Cut back on sugar, fats, fast foods and sodas for 30 days*

Day 1 Define your goal. Did you complete your goal? If no, why not?

_____

_____

_____

Day 2 Define your goal. Did you complete your goal? If no, why not?

_____

_____

_____

Day 3 Define your goal. Did you complete your goal? If no, why not? ____

_____

_____

_____

Day 4 Define your goal. Did you complete your goal? If no, why not?

_____

_____

_____

Day 5 Define your goal. Did you complete your goal? If no, why not?

_____

_____

_____

Day 6 Define your goal. Did you complete your goal? If no, why not?

_____

_____

_____

Day 7 Define your goal. Did you complete your goal? If no, why not?

_____

_____

_____

Day 8 Define your goal. Did you complete your goal? If no, why not?

_____

_____

_____

Day 9 Define your goal. Did you complete your goal? If no, why not?

_____

_____

_____

Day 10 Define your goal. Did you complete your goal? If no, why not?

_____

_____

_____

Day 11 Define your goal. Did you complete your goal? If no, why not?

_____

_____

_____

Day 12 Define your goal. Did you complete your goal? If no, why not?

_____

_____

_____

Day 13 Define your goal. Did you complete your goal? If no, why not?

_____

_____

_____

Day 14 Define your goal. Did you complete your goal? If no, why not?

_____

_____

_____

Day 15 Define your goal. Did you complete your goal? If no, why not?

_____

_____

_____

Day 16 Define your goal. Did you complete your goal? If no, why not?

_____

_____

_____

Day 17 Define your goal. Did you complete your goal? If no, why not?

_____

_____

_____

Day 18 Define your goal. Did you complete your goal? If no, why not?

_____

_____

_____

Day 19 Define your goal. Did you complete your goal? If no, why not?

_____

_____

_____

Day 20 Define your goal. Did you complete your goal? If no, why not?

_____

_____

_____

Day 21 Define your goal. Did you complete your goal? If no, why not?

_____

_____

_____

Day 22 Define your goal. Did you complete your goal? If no, why not?

_____

_____

_____

Day 23 Define your goal. Did you complete your goal? If no, why not?

_____

_____

_____

Day 24 Define your goal. Did you complete your goal? If no, why not?

_____

_____

_____

Day 25 Define your goal. Did you complete your goal? If no, why not?

_____

_____

_____

Day 26 Define your goal. Did you complete your goal? If no, why not?

_____

_____

_____

Day 27 Define your goal. Did you complete your goal? If no, why not?

_____

_____

_____

Day 28 Define your goal. Did you complete your goal? If no, why not?

_____

_____

_____

Day 29 Define your goal. Did you complete your goal? If no, why not?

_____

_____

_____

Day 30 Define your goal. Did you complete your goal? If no, why not?

_____

_____

_____

Pause but do not park

As we embrace change in our lives, I want to encourage each of you to pause, but do not park.

Remember to always celebrate Christ during Christmas because Jesus Christ is the reason for the season, and any other season that there is or change in your life. I want to ask you to remember this please, pause but do not park.

While pausing is necessary some times, parking may need navigating. As you enter a new year, a new phase in your life whether it be through marriage, a new church, a new neighborhood, a new job, a new school, any life changes or a new year, whatever it is just pause, but do not park. Whatever you do remember again please only pause, but do not park. Whatever you reflect on, you can pause, but do not park.
Read Psalms 107:43

Enjoy your journey

What we do on our journey depends on the choices we make. Whether you are sitting, driving or riding your journey has been predestined and prepared.

If you are just sitting, you may need to reevaluate your journey. If you happen to be riding along, make sure that you know where you are going, and whom you are traveling with. If you are driving, be certain that you have your road map, you are somewhat familiar with the road, and you know exactly when to stop, go, which way to turn, when to slow down, if the road curves, or where to park.

If work is your journey, you should love to work, and love what you do while you work. The only way to enjoy on your journey is to have joy on your journey. Your journey should include joy. Full joy is enjoyed when you include Jesus. The only way to fully enjoy your journey is to have joy in Jesus.

Read John 17:13

What's in your pity party?

Pity parties are allowed just don't adjust to them. Your place of pity can determine your negative or positive attitude. There are negatives and positives in pity. However, I can definitely tell you that there are more positives than negatives in your pity party. If you are in a pit, there is an excavation going on. To excavate means to dig a hole or cavity. A cavity or hole has an opening. So if something is open, there is nothing blocking it. Some time even though a hole is open and may be void, it may contain nothing, but in order for you to have a pity party you must occupy the pit, or reside in it. Since the pit is not your home, and you cannot remain in the pit, remember even if there are negatives, and your pity party holds you in a tight grip, there are more positives than negatives in your pity party.

Positives
Prayer
Positive
Perseverance
Purpose
Patience
Process
Proof
Power
Prosperity
Perfect
Peace
Promise
Protection
Promotion
Provision

Passion
Plan
Present
Polished
Potential

<u>NEGATIVES</u>
Pressures
Problems
Persecutions
Pits
Pity
Past
Pooped
Peculiar*

*Peculiar may not always be a negative

Read Psalms 107:4-8

The Adversary is not your Ace Boon Coon

Remember the enemy will 'always' be your adversary and never your ace. Who is your adversary? I'm so glad you asked. It could be an acquaintenance that you only conversate with. It could be someone only pretending to be your friend. It could be anyone who attacks your achievements whether that achievement is personal, private or professional. You see the adversary does not have your back, the adversary is selfish, and is not for you, or for anything that is HONEST, RIGHT or TRUE. The adversary always SEEKS to KILL, STEAL and DESTROY you in EVERY AREA where God has ORDAINED OBEDIENCE. The adversary wants to KILL, STEAL and DESTROY your integrity, Godly spirit, your Godly relationships, Godly thinking, your good name, your character, your marriage, your peace, your good attitude, your health, your faith and even you.
Read I Peter 5:8

Waiting for God when you are being wronged

There are times when waiting for God seems impossible. Satan wants you to fight, fret, fear, faint, fall, and lose your faith while waiting for God to fix whoever or whatever your concern is. No matter how large or small, waiting for God can be uncomfortable, and some times may seem unnecessary especially if you are being wronged. Waiting requires you to withstand and stand still until the wind stops blowing. Wrong never wins no matter what. When you wait for God you will win. If you wait for God he can help you, because He wants to work on your behalf.

While you must wait some times, look at these words in waiting and their meanings:
a-first letter of the alphabet indicates a function
I-describes the person-self

wait-to delay
gnaw-showing anxiety
in –located inside or within
at-indicates the presence of or occurrence
win-success, earn
want-to have a lack or to require
nag-complain, annoyance, constant irritant
ant-impatient for action or activity
twain-two, couple, pair
wit-ability to amuse, to come to know, to learn
wag-shake, to be in motion
wig-covering for your head
wing-an extension
gait –walk, step, pace-the way you walk or move

Read Job 14:14, Isaiah 40:31, Lamentations 3:25-26, Psalms 1:5-6, Psalms 37:7-9, Psalms 40:1 and Ephesians 6:13

Don't give Satan access

Be careful what you allow in you in your spirit, because it will affect what comes out of you. What you allow in your space will affect everything about you and around you. If you are motivated by sin, you will never be satisfied and you will be weakened. When you are motivated by the Savior, you will be secure and strengthened-*read Proverbs 14:32-22, Matthew 23:28, Romans 8:5-8*

Take time out to be Thankful

Comfort or change keeps everyone thankful

Sometimes we just need to say "have a thankful day, take time to be thankful, don't ask God for anything, but thank Him for everything."
Read Psalms 30:12, Psalms 44:8, Psalms 75:1, Psalms 100:4, Psalms 116:17, Psalms 118:28, Psalms 150:6, II Corinthians 9:11, I Thessalonians 5:18 and Colossians 2:7
(Thank you to my cousin Karen)

Stay in the Crosswalk

If you are looking for God, stay in the crosswalk. The crosswalk is the intersection between heaven and hell.

What's in the crosswalk?
God's Provision
God's Protection
God's Promises
God's Power
God's Peace
God's Perfection
God's Purpose
God's Possibilities
God's Plan
God's Partnership

Read John 14:6

Triumph in Trouble

In order to build up some times things have to be torn down. Under the rubble you must hold on and not be moved by what is said or not said, don't become weary or bend by the ways of those who have no understanding of the trouble.

There may even be times when you have to pray for others understanding to be opened, and you continue on and do right. *Galatians 6:9 reminds us that not to be moved or weary in doing good because if you give in or if you give up, you cannot reap the benefits from your labor and the seeds that you have sown.* Men lie, cheat, steal, cut down, hate, manipulate etc., God does not and will never do any of that.

When we do our portion, we know God will do His part, because he has our best interest at heart. Satan and our haters do not. Since God has our best interest at heart, He is constantly and continuously working on our behalf. Remember you can always trust God in trouble who promises comfort, commitment, compassion, and covering. Never put your trust in man who plants criticism, crisis, cant's, condemnation, corruption and confusion-re*ad Psalms 25:2-3, Psalms 118:8, 1 Peter 4:12 and 1 Corinthians 14:33*

A day to do dat=TODAY

A day to just smile-_read Proverbs 15:14 and Proverbs 16:20_

A day to let your light shine for God-_read Matthew 5:16_

A day to stand-_read Ephesians 4:14_

A day to spread the word-_read I Thessalonians 1:8_

A day to lift up a standard-_read I Corinthians 10:13_

A day to stir up your gift-_read 2 Timothy 1:6_

A day to be still and know God-_read Psalms 46:10_

A day to study God's word-_read 2 Timothy 2:15_

A day to submit to God's will-_read James 4:7_

Influence or Impact

Are we influencing or impacting the world for Christ, or is the world influencing or impacting us to change. Be determined to make impacts that will influence the world. I believe it was Gandhi who said, "Be the change you wish to see in this world." I feel we should strive to influence the world, and make such an impact for God's glory. Most of the time we allow the world to influence us, and this can definitely impact the world. The world's influence can change us, and often it influences us to change, but not for God's glory. We should be so determined to be the change that we want to see in the world today.

In order to hear or receive an instruction you must REMOVE interruptions and outside interferences and influences, that can invade your obedience to God's will and way-*read Proverbs 21:3 and read Matthew 5:16*

Hope in between your destiny

I was working on something for one of my brothers, and I asked my daughter about this title "House of Hope." My daughter responded back with "hope in between your destiny." I must say that hope is in your destiny. You always have hope in your destiny and even in between your destiny, you can hope. God has told us to walk by faith and not by sight, and that is exactly what hope is. There is always hope-R*ead Hebrews 11:1* (Thank you to my daughter-D. Ashley)

You got to laugh

Don't cry before you laugh that it's over. Don't cry in your battle, God has something better. LAUGH IT OUT!
Read-They that sow in tears shall reap in joy-Psalms 126:5

CHOICES STUDY GUIDE WORKSHEET

Look at each of the choices listed and make a disciplined effort to practice the positive choice daily. Write down any struggle/s you may have had with practicing the positive choice.

Faith—vs fear

_____

_____

_____

Gratitude—vs—grumbling

_____

_____

_____

Worship—vs—worry

_____

_____

_____

Excellence—vs—excuses

_____

_____

_____

Discipline—vs—disobedience

_____

_____

_____

Committed—vs—complacent

_____

_____

_____

Hope –vs—helplessness

_____

_____

_____

Don't blow your covering

"Check the location where Jesus is before you get caught with the wrong Person, at the wrong Place, in the wrong Position". Keeping good godly character and a good name is better than being with the wrong person, at the wrong place, in the wrong position, or just at the wrong place, with the wrong person and definitely at the wrong time for any reason. Whether it is to satisfy your own selfishness, or just being too casual, too careless, or because you think it feels good. <u>Wrong should always make us feel uncomfortable no matter what it is</u>. Remember this! There is no such thing as just FRIENDLY INTENTIONS. We should RUN away from and stay away from anything that causes us to be tempted, tricked or trapped into SIN or "slip" from under our covering. You may never get caught (so you think) but God does see all that we do at all times no matter where we are, how we think we are hiding what we do, or whom we are with. When you are in the wrong location, you always have to sneak around, you become a prisoner to your own wrongs, and you actually shackle yourself. When you are doing right or in the right location, you will be free and have peace in <u>every</u> situation with no shame.

If you ever have to sneak
You will definitely sink
Satan will seek you
And you certainly will stink.

Read Luke 23:41

Get your swag on

God gives you a gift everyday. You can accomplish anything with God. You are worth so much to God. You can relax in God's blessings. In God everything always works out. God provides you His best each day.
Read Psalms 27:3 and Proverbs 14:26

Let's look at certainty

You must be sensitive to the will of God so you can receive what the Holy Spirit speaks into you. When you receive instructions from God, you will have certainty in your direction.
Read Luke 1:4

Accept your assignment

Accept your assignment to do God's will so God's grace does not have to apprehend or arrest you. We cannot alter God's agenda. When you accept God's will, you will always have the grace of God. You can control your action, but you cannot change or control God's agenda. When God appoints you, he approves you. You cannot argue with God's appointment. All He asks that we do is to acknowledge Him, and we can be assured that God's grace will assist us along the way of our assignment-*read Jeremiah 1:5 and II Corinthians 12:9*

So how long will you do wrong?

How long will you continue to do wrong?

Don't continue in unforgiveness. God provides forgiveness for you through Jesus blood.

Are you faking? You won't be making it, if you are faking it.

You either cannot or don't want to do right.

Remember: You will reap what you sow.

If you are continuing to do wrong you are:

- **UNCOMFORTABLE**
- **UNFORGIVEN**
- **UNRULY**
- **No understanding**
- **No respect**

You will never have any peace
Until your wrong you cease!

Proverbs 26:11 says this: If you continue to do wrong it is like a dog
that vomits and returns to it.

Standing on Bended Knees

There are times when the storm of life is so strong and your knees are down, but you can still stand even when your knees are bent down to the ground. While standing may even require some assistance, you may have to learn how to fight on your knees.
Read Ephesians 3:14

Greetings and Goodbye

In some instances there are only these two words that are necessary to say.

<u>*Greetings to*</u>**: Holiness, Faith, Hope, Love, Joy, Peace, Happiness, Knowledge, Victory, Grace, Mercy, Covering, Righteous, Accord, Prayer, Today, Faith, Trust, Can, Giving, Encouragement, Prosperity, Health, Blessing, Wisdom, and Victory**

<u>*Goodbye to:*</u> **Fear, Sickness, Doubt, Worry, Can't, Hate/Haters, Frowns, Fighting, Past Failures, Insecurity, Greed, Guilt, Past, Messiness, Discord, Discontent, Gossip and Selfishness**

Read Proverbs 3:5-6, Luke 18:27, John 3:16, Philippians 4:13 and I Peter 5:7

Watch your words

There is truly life and death in your tongue. We must watch our words and speak life. Never speak negative. Your walk and your talk must be the same. You cannot say one thing with your lips, and do another with your life. Always speak positive words because your tongue sets the stage between your stepping stone and your stumbling block**.**
Read Psalms 19:14, Proverbs 18:21, and Philippians 4:13

Don't just do better, but do right

There is no such thing as doing a little wrong, because wrong is NEVER right, and you can never explain it. Continual wrong makes you a deceiver, hypocrite, liar, and counterfeit Christian. You cannot explain wrong and only do better. Better is not good enough. Your choices today could ruin your character, and cause you to crack, be crushed and become confused and most of all lose your Christian witness. You must do right not just better. **Remember this: Don't just do better, don't just do good, but do right.**

Don't be a Counterfeit Christian

Don't just do better do right
Don't just do good either!
Don't just do better that is not good enough!
You must do right!

Read Jeremiah 17:5-11 and Proverbs 21:3

A Day to Smile

Each day that God gives you on earth to open your eyes again, smile. Think of it this way that you have another opportunity today, and another chance, so smile. Even if you feel like you are peeling apart, loosing all control of your normal calm demeanor, or just want to cry when everything seems to be going wrong, smile.

A smile can radiate so much energy in your body. When your feet hit the floor look in the mirror and smile. Practice this every day. Raise your arms, spread out your fingers and move your feet and smile. Your entire body will begin to glow. In fact, if you smile long enough, your eyes, ears and tummy will blush, and you just might break into a laugh.

Since you cannot frown and smile at the same time, everyday is a day to smile. Smile long, smile hard, smile wide, smile big, just smile. Below are reasons to smile each day.

- God breaths another day to you
- God allows your ears to hear your alarm clock
- God opens your eyes to see your way
- God prepares a path for your feet and legs to walk
- God gives you access to your arms and hands to use
- God unlocks your mouth and makes it available
- God benefits you with taste and smell
- God provides everything you need everyday

Each day when you open your eyes remember God is smiling at you. Smile back at Him, and say thank you to God for the day He has given to you. ***Read Psalms 118:24***

Daily Divine Inspirations from God

You must turn from sin, in order to see God's Son—*read Romans 6:5-18*

Don't let feelings manipulate your mind, and don't be tricked by your flesh because you just might trip—*read James 1:14*

Always remember to pray, and to be careful in everything you ask God for—*read Philippians 4:4-11*

Failure is not an option faith is—*read Hebrews 11:1-3*

Instead of being an instigator, be an imitator of Christ—*read I Corinthians 11:1*

Trust in God's promises and experience God's blessings-God always keeps His promises for His plans and purposes—*read Numbers 23:19 and Proverbs 3:5-6*

Let your inner beauty show more than your outer beauty shines—*read II Corinthians 4:16-18*

Don't carry burdens, they will turn into bags on you—*read Matthew 11:28-30 and I Peter 5:7*

Maintain a childlike quality and restrain from childish character—*read Matthew 18:3-6*

God will turn your tears and fears to cheers—*read Psalms 30:11-12, Isaiah 61:31 and Jeremiah 29:11-13*

It may rain but you don't have to ruin or run—*read Hosea 6:3*

We always want God to show up for us, but we don't stand out for Him—*read 2 Chronicles 16:9*

Remember to pray always, always pray, not just pray also—*read Luke 18:1, I Thessalonians 5:17 and II Thessalonians 1:11*

God provides peace and power you just put in the prayer and the praise—*read Isaiah 40:29, Psalms 47, Psalms 150, Romans 12:12 and II Thessalonians 3:16*

Big things are easily seen, but little things mean a lot more, and are very much appreciated—*read Psalms 37:16*

When God says no, He will put a period. Don't change it to a comma because when you do, you invite drama. Learn from your past, so you can live for God in the present—*read Philippians 3:13-14*

You usually cannot control the fire, but in holiness you will not be consumed by the flames-*read Isaiah 43:2*

Don't take risks in the present because it could ruin your future-*read Jeremiah 29:1, Job 23:10 and Proverbs 16:1-3*

Service does include being a servant-read *Psalms 116:16*

If the blind can see possibilities, why do those who are not blind see so many impossibilities—*read Luke 18:27*

Let go of your shackles so you can shout-*read Exodus 15:2*

Follow your faith and not your flesh—*read Romans 8:8*

Don't walk on the edge because you will fall—*read Galatians 5:19-21*

God can change your woes to wows—*read Psalms 33:8-9*

You may overlook God's word, but you cannot ignore God—*read Haggai 1:7-9 and 2:17-19*

God has interest in your rest—*read Matthew 11:28-29*

Look at the word hear and let your ear hear the word of the Lord—*read Matthew 13:19 and Revelation 13:9*

God will give you a heads up even when things are upside down—*read Matthew 6:8 and John 13:1*

Walk in the light not in darkness—*read Psalms 119:105*

Pursue excellence don't practice excuses—*read Luke 14:18*

Don't be discouraged in discipline—there is delight in correction—*read Proverbs 3:12*

God uses difficulty to design us for our destiny—*read Psalms 34:3-8 and Ephesians 6:10-11*

Why do we pay a lot attention to everything else and a little attention to God's word—*read James 4:10 and John 15:5*

God is the leader you be the follower of Him and you will not be lead astray, and He will take care of you-*read Psalms 23:1, 27:11, 143:10, John 8:12 and I Peter 2:21*

There are benefits if you don't breakdown-*read Psalms 68:19 and Hebrews 10:23*

You cannot control God's will, but you can control your actions in God's way—*read Romans 12:2, Hebrews 13:21, Philippians 2:13*

You may have to suffer or struggle but the storm won't last—*read Mark 4:37-40*

Don't get so involved and consumed in the party that you forget to dance—*read Psalms 30:11-12*

You may be on the right road, but you can't just stand there. To get to another level you must move. *read Matthew 7:7-8 and 13-14 and 24*

Be spirit led not people pressured and do not be manipulated—*read Jeremiah 17:5 and 7*

You don't have to fight with the devil because he is already defeated-*read Deuteronomy 2:33, 2 Chronicles 20:15 and James 4:7*

Deal with difficulties and give God glory in it—*read Jeremiah 29:11*

When you are a new creature in Christ, you must know what to leave behind—*read II Corinthians 5:17*

Remember this! Some things are so worthless. Some things are less worthy and not even worth talking or thinking about. Don't expect more, but give less. Never give more and expect less or just settle for whatever-*read Proverbs 6:12-14 Proverbs 16:27-28 II Timothy 2:20-22*

Don't allow misery to be your company—(Example: People who have madness don't want you to have happiness; those who hate don't want you to love; those who live in the past don't want you to live in the present; those who doubt don't want you to believe; those who are disobedient don't want you to be obedient; those who curse don't want you to bless)-*read Romans 8:1-2 and Philippians 4:8-9*

If you wait for God, you will win!
Read Job 14:14, Psalms 37:7-9 Ephesians 6:13 Lamentations 3:25-26 Psalms 1:5-6, and Psalms 40:1

Do you need a reason to be thankful?
Read Psalms 136:1

There is always a low before you reach your high place- read Isaiah 57:14-15
(Thank you to my daughter)

I'm moving on up and it is going to be greater later-read Haggai 2:9
(Thank you to my daughter)

God always has flowers for you. He flowers you with favor, faith, fitness and fervency, but your focus must stay on Him.

God's flowered favor of faith, fitness, and fervency

Favor of Faith

For your focus on Him

Read-2 Corinthians 5:7, James 2:17 and 22, and Hebrews 11:1

Favor of Fitness

For your foundation (your body)

Read-1 Corinthians 3:11, Ephesians 2:20-21 and 1 Timothy 6:19

Favor of Fervency

For your flame (spirit)

Read-Romans 12:11, Colossians 4:12 and I Peter 1:22

(Thank you to Sonja for the word fervent)

"Grow don't just glow – Grow" (AWww/God)

God can change your Panic to Picnic (to Praise)

I have experienced some panic, that I never ever would think of a picnic. I couldn't even begin to think of a picnic, or even see the picnic in the panic. Panic is no picnic, but God always provides just what you need just when you need it, because he already knows your need. I had sent this text message out several months prior to October 28, 2010, but on this date my husband said it should say "God can change your panic to praise". Well this is another awesome message from God. "Praise God in your panic because God can change your panic to praise."

Read Philippians 4:8, I Thessalonians 5:16-18 and Hebrews 13:15

(Thank you to my husband)

Walking with God 7 days a week

Monday
Make it a magnifying, merry, marvelous, mindful, merciful, meek and mustard-seed Monday.
Read Psalms 34:3, Proverbs 15:15, I Peter 2:9, Hebrews 2:6, Joel 2:13, Matthew 5:5 and Matthew 13:31

Tuesday
This is a tasteful, trusting, triumphant and thankful Tuesday.
Read Psalms34:8, Psalms 37:5, Proverbs 3:5, II Corinthians 2:14, and Psalms 95:2

Wednesday
Walk in a wondrous, working, watchful, worshipping wisdom word Wednesday.
Read II Corinthians 5:7, Psalms 75:1, James 1:25, II Timothy 4:5, John 9:31, Psalms 119:11 and Proverbs 3:13

Thursday
Have a testifying, tasteful, trusting, triumphant and thankful Thursday.
Read Psalms 34:8, Psalms 37:5, Proverbs 3:5, II Corinthians 2:14, and Psalms 95:2

Friday
Have a focused, favorable, fruitful, fantastic and Faith-filled Friday.
Read Psalms 30:5, Colossians 1:10 and Hebrews 11:1

Saturday
Savor a Seeking, Sharing, Strengthened, Sowing, Spiritual, Sufficient, Submissive Saturday.
Read Psalms 126:6, Matthew 6:33, 2 Corinthians 9:8, 2 Corinthians 12:9, Philippians 4:13, and Hebrews 11:6

Sunday
Submit to a Settled, Serving, Self-controlled, Self confident, Steadfast, Striving, Successful Sunday.
Read Proverbs 16:3, Luke 21:14, Romans 12:11, Galatians 5:23, Titus 1:8, 2 Peter 1:6 and Colossians 1:29

A Woman walking with God—A 30 day Journal

Find a scripture to the following statements for each day
Pray over the statement and the scripture (Ex. Day 1: Ask God to help
you follow His will).
Be sure to journal your thoughts regarding each day's scripture
On Day 27 go back and read your journal notes from Day 1

Day 1 A woman following the will of God.

_____
_____
_____

Day 2 A woman submitting to the work of God.

_____
_____
_____

Day 3 A woman listening to the word of God.

_____
_____
_____

Day 4 A woman obedient to the will of God.

_____
_____
_____

Day 5 A woman acknowledging the plan of God.

_____

_____

_____

Day 6 A woman praying to God regarding His will.

_____

_____

_____

Day 7 A woman worshipping God in His will.

_____

_____

_____

Day 8 A woman praising God for His word.

_____

_____

_____

Day 9 A woman walking in the ways of God.

_____

_____

_____

Day 10 A woman committed to the will of God.

_____

_____

_____

Day 11 A woman encouraged by the word of God

_____

_____

_____

Day 12 A woman successful in God.

_____

_____

_____

Day 13 A woman waiting for an answer from God.

_____

_____

_____

Day 14 A woman dependant on God.

_____

_____

_____

Day 15 A woman seeking the will of God.

_____

_____

_____

Day 16 A woman available for the work of God.

_____

_____

_____

Day 17 A woman who has time to spend with God.

_____

_____

_____

Day 18 A woman sensitive to the will of God.

_____

_____

_____

Day 19 A woman thankful to God.

_____

_____

_____

Day 20 A woman satisfied to do the will of God.

_____

_____

_____

Day 21 A woman influencing others for God.

_____

_____

_____

Day 22 A woman serving God.

_____

_____

_____

Day 23 A woman trusting God.

_____

_____

_____

Day 24 A woman faithful to God.

_____

_____

_____

Day 25 A woman studying the word of God.

_____

_____

_____

Day 26 A woman accepting the will of God.

_____

_____

_____

Day 27 A woman motivated by the word of God.

_____

_____

_____

Day 28 A woman sharing the word of God.

_____

_____

_____

Day 29 A woman changing for the purpose of God.

_____

_____

_____

Day 30 A woman fasting for God's deliverance.

_____

_____

_____

Walking with God 30 days—A Journal

- *Each week write out your goal/s you want to accomplish*
- *Is this a goal/s that God wants you to accomplish?*
- *Pray over your goals*
- *Be sure to journal your goal/s weekly to observe your progress*
- *Keep a journal if you accomplished or did not accomplish the goal/s*
- *Indicate reason why you did not accomplish your goal/s.*
- *Determine if you can complete any unfinished goal/s within the next month.*
- *Are the goals obtainable within the next 30 days or the next six months?*

Week 1

_____
_____
_____
_____
_____

Week 2

_____
_____
_____
_____
_____

Week 3

_____
_____
_____
_____
_____

Week 4

_____
_____
_____
_____
_____

Week 5

_____
_____
_____
_____
_____

12 month Calendar walking with God—in God's will, way, work and word

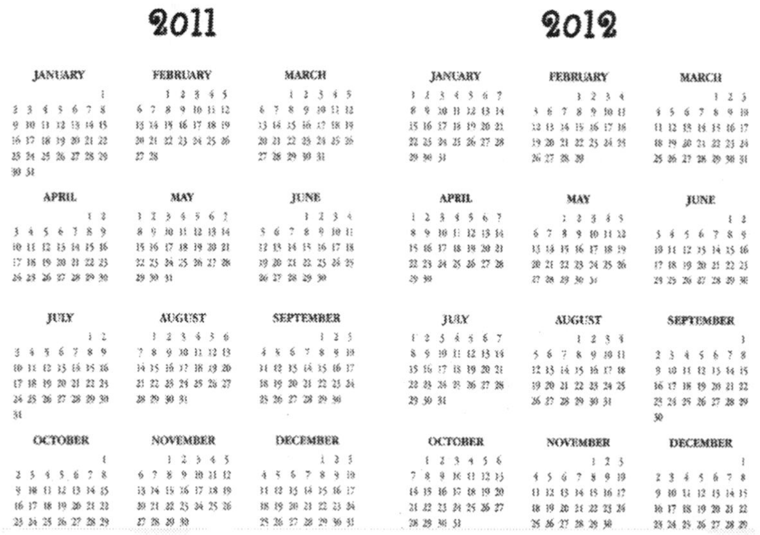
2011
2012
JANUARY
FEBRUARY
MARCH
APRIL
MAY
JUNE
JULY
AUGUST
SEPTEMBER
OCTOBER
NOVEMBER
DECEMBER

Look at the words listed each month; read the scripture/s, journal how this relates to you walking w/God and journal your progress each week for the entire month.

Did you accomplish the assignment for the month? If no, why not and can you complete next month?

January-Willing
Read Jeremiah 32: 38-41 and Hebrews 6:3

Week 1

____

____

____

____

____

Week 2

_____
_____
_____
_____
_____

Week 3

_____
_____
_____
_____
_____

Week 4

_____
_____
_____
_____
_____

February-Waiting
Read Genesis 49:18, Psalms 27:10, Psalms 37:9 and Isaiah 40:31

Week 1

_____
_____
_____
_____
_____

Week 2

_____

_____

_____

_____

_____

Week 3

_____

_____

_____

_____

_____

Week 4

_____

_____

_____

_____

_____

March-Watching
Read Psalms 102:7, Proverbs 8:34, Matthew 25:13, Mark 13:37 and Colossians 4:2

Week 1

_____

_____

_____

_____

_____

Week 2

_____
_____
_____
_____
_____

Week 3

_____
_____
_____
_____
_____

Week 4

_____
_____
_____
_____
_____

April-Walking
Read Psalms 119:1 and 3 and 2 Corinthians 5:7

Week 1

_____
_____
_____
_____
_____

Week 2

_____
_____
_____
_____
_____

Week 3

_____
_____
_____
_____
_____

Week 4

_____
_____
_____
_____
_____

May-Working/Worker
Read Isaiah 1:19, John 9:4 and James 2:17

Week 1

_____
_____
_____
_____
_____

Week 2

_____
_____
_____
_____
_____

Week 3

_____
_____
_____
_____
_____

Week 4

_____
_____
_____
_____
_____

June-Not Wavering
Read Romans 4:20 and Hebrews 10:23

Week 1

_____
_____
_____
_____
_____

Week 2

_____
_____
_____
_____
_____

Week 3

_____
_____
_____
_____
_____

Week 4

_____
_____
_____
_____
_____

July-Wisdom
Read Proverbs 1:2, Proverbs 2:6, Proverbs 21:30, Luke 21:15 and Colossians 2:3

Week 1

_____
_____
_____
_____
_____

Week 2

_____
_____
_____
_____
_____

Week 3

_____
_____
_____
_____
_____

Week 4

_____
_____
_____
_____
_____

August-Witness
Read Proverbs 14:5, I John 5:7-9

Week 1

_____
_____
_____
_____
_____

Week 2

_____
_____
_____
_____
_____

Week 3

_____
_____
_____
_____
_____

Week 4

_____
_____
_____
_____
_____

September-Withstands
Read Luke 21:15 and I Peter 5:9

Week 1

_____
_____
_____
_____
_____

Week 2

_____
_____
_____
_____
_____

Week 3

_____
_____
_____
_____
_____

Week 4

_____
_____
_____
_____
_____

October-Worshipper
Read Psalms 96:9, Psalms 99:5, Psalms 119:2 and John 4:24

Week 1

_____
_____
_____
_____
_____

Week 2

_____
_____
_____
_____
_____

Week 3

_____
_____
_____
_____
_____

Week 4

_____
_____
_____
_____
_____

November-Whole
Read Jeremiah 32:41 and Psalms 119:2

Week 1

_____
_____
_____
_____
_____

Week 2

_____
_____
_____
_____
_____

Week 3

_____
_____
_____
_____
_____

Week 4

_____
_____
_____
_____
_____

December-Ask God what's next?
Read Matthew 6:6-8 and 32-33, Matthew 7:7, John 11:22, James 1:5

Week 1

_____
_____
_____
_____
_____

Week 2

_____
_____
_____
_____
_____

Week 3

_____
_____
_____
_____
_____

Week 4

_____
_____
_____
_____
_____

SINGLES STUDY GUIDE WORKSHEET QUESTIONS

Singles Worksheet Questions

1. Do you know your God-given purpose?

2. Do you use your time/money wisely?

3. Do you spend time with any Christian single group?

4. Are you utilizing your purpose for God? If no-why not?

5. Are you being productive in your free time?

6. Regarding God's word, are there things you need to be disciplined about?

7. Are you seeking to do God's will diligently, or just your own to do list?

8. Are you being careless if you are idle?

9. Do you demand others to respect your temple?

10. Do you feel obligated to participate in activities just so you will not be alone? Are they worthwhile, worthless or worthy of sharing?

11. Do you respect others time, and do you respect your own time?

12. Do you have any short term goals that you can accomplish in one year or less?

13. Are you satisfied with your current single status? If no, why not?

14. Do you have a budget, a savings, any investments?

15. Is your spending out of control because you feel you don't have to report to anyone?

16. Do you go to the movies, shopping or out to dinner alone? If no, why not?

17. Because you are single, do you over spend?

18. Are you trusting totally in the Lord and seeking His will and guidance for your single life?

19. Are you afraid to stand alone and not go along with the crowd?

20. Are you comfortable being single, when others may consider it as different?

21. What do you do for fun?

22. Who do you spend your free time with?

23. Do you feel you have your life in order according to God's will?

MARRIED COUPLES STUDY GUIDE WORKSHEET QUESTIONS

Married Couples Worksheet Questions

1. What do your wedding vows mean to you today?

2. Do you put your spouse and your marriage first before your family?

3. Do you express to others/outsiders about your marriage relationship during casual conversations, or to express your feelings, beliefs, concerns, questions and your opinions, or do you keep that within your marriage and share with your spouse?

4. Even though you may have different interests, do you spend time equally with each other doing something your spouse enjoys on a regular basis?

5. Do you discuss concerns with your spouse first, or do you talk to someone else about it?

6. Do you celebrate every marriage anniversary together alone? What do you do?

7. Do you wear your rings? If not, why not? (Do you remember you made a "vow" with this ring I thee wed?)

8. Do you consider your marriage as a partnership, relationship or companionship?

9. Do you feel your spouse has helped you become a better individual in some way? Do they know it?

10. Do you thank or express appreciation to your spouse regularly for no special reason (in private only, in public, or both equally)

11. Do you go on vacation together separately from children or family/friends etc?

12. What do you do on the weekends together?

13. Do you pray together daily?

14. Do you spend enormous amount of time w/single peers, former friends, old classmates? Why?

15. When you have a disagreement, do you apologize to your spouse even if you were not wrong?

16. Do you discuss your day with your spouse, and also allow your spouse to discuss their day?

17. Have you and your spouse ever undertaken and completed a huge project together. If so what were your struggles during the project? How did you overcome them?

18. Do you exercise together? What do you do?

19. Do you remember where you met your spouse, your first date, and how long you dated before you were married?

20. Do you discuss any of your bills and money matters outside of your marriage circle with your friends, family or co-workers?

21. How do you encourage your spouse? Do you encourage them regularly/consistently?

22. Are you in agreement with your spouse regarding values in your marriage?

WAITING FOR GOD WHEN YOU ARE BEING WRONGED STUDY GUIDE WORKSHEET QUESTIONS

Waiting for God when you are being wronged Worksheet Questions

1. What was your initial reaction to discovering you had been wronged by someone?

2. Did you confront them/will you? If yes? What was their response?

3. Have you been wronged by the same person more than once? What has been your response?

4. Have they confessed they were wrong? Did they apologize? What was your response?

5. Will you bring it up to them again what they are doing to you is wrong, even if they never acknowledge it, and never apologize to you, or do not seem remorseful for wronging you?

6. Can you forgive them even though they may still be doing wrong to you, and you know about it?

7. If an individual never admits to doing wrong, and continue to do wrong, and lies about it to you, should you confront them?

8. Have you ever confronted someone about a wrong they have done or continue doing to you, and they act like it is you who are wrong for asking them about what they are doing? How did you handle this?

9. Do you look for opportunities to get back at the person who has wronged you, or who may still be wronging you?

10. Do you believe the person who has wronged you suffers?

11. Can you ever trust an individual who has wronged you over and over with no apologies?

12. Do you always think about the wrong the person did and they might do it again?

13. What does God say about vengeance?

14. What does God say about forgiveness?

15. Have you ever wronged anyone? How did you respond to them?

Christ sacrificed His life for us, and we cannot begin to imagine all that He suffered for us in exchange for our sins. If we understood what Christ endured for us, we would undertake/unselfishly to endeavor to live a life for Him.

Be still and know that I am God

~ Psalm 46:10

With Jesus, it only took 1 cross and 3 nails for our forgiveness.

If you do not know Jesus Christ as your personal Savior, I invite you to pray this prayer and accept Him now.

I acknowledge that I have sinned, I ask you to forgive me for my sins and come into my heart. I accept you as my personal Savior, and I believe you died on the cross for my sins. Help me daily as I strive to live for you. Thank you that the tomb is empty today, and you were raised for me with all power.

If you prayed this prayer and you made a decision to accept Jesus Christ as your personal Savior, write your name and today's date below:

Your name

Today's date

Scripture references: John 3:16-17, Romans 10:9, I John 5:15-16

Requests for information, to purchase additional books, or to schedule an event contact:

Phone: 214/944-5556 then press #1

Or email at: jjmrsjack@gmail.com

Available at Amazon.com and Barnes & Noble.com

Upcoming inspirations:

- Virtues
- Soul source
- Running and crying in Faith and Joy
- Clean up or clean out
- Words of wisdom from God for a woman of God
- Living large but who is in charge
- I'll be on my best behavior
- Stir up the gift not the guilt
- I'm trying to be better than that
- I thought of you
- Single, saved, sanctified, satisfied and seriously serving God
- Healing from the inside out
- There is a script in your prescription
- A better path
- God is a giver
- You don't know my story
- Are you a beggar, borrower, bummer, or a blesser?
- Don't be trifling
- You can't afford not to tithe
- Why can't you let go of your mess
- You do not have to fight the devil
- You got benefits
- Risks cause wrecks
- Total commitment
- What happens when things go KABOOM!
- Division, Revision, Provision, Envision, Supervision, but not television